The HIGH-FLYING WORLD of KITES

by Ray Paprocki

Willowisp
Press®

To my spirited Anastasia—
who makes me smile

PHOTO CREDITS: **Lois Debolt,** pages 2 (top and middle right), 4 (all except middle right), 6 (bottom left), 7, 14 (top and bottom right), 15 (left and right), 16 (top right), 17 (top right), 18, 19 (bottom right), 20 (top, middle, and bottom right), 21, 22 (all), 23 (upper middle left), 25 (middle left), 29 (bottom left, top), 30 (top and bottom right), **Aunt Cassie and Uncle Wilbert,** pages 2 (bottom left), 4 (middle right), 6 (top right), 14 (left), 16 (bottom left), 19 (bottom and middle left), 23 (lower middle left), 24, 25 (bottom left), 26 (three bottom photos), 30 (bottom left), **The Bettmann Archive,** page 9 (all), **Go Fly A Kite, Inc.,** page 5, **Oscar Bailey,** pages 15 (center), 16 (bottom right), 17 (top left), 23 (bottom left), **Mike Keating and Fred Bell,** pages 2 (bottom right), 6 (the four individual kites), 8, 12-13, 19 (top left), 28 (both). Front and back cover photos and photos on pages 17 (bottom), 20 (bottom left), 23 (top left, bottom right), 25 (top left, bottom right), 26 (top right), 27, 29 (bottom right), courtesy of **Into The Wind,** a mail order catalog of kites and kite materials available by writing to: 1408 Pearl Street, Boulder, CO, 80302.

Illustrations on pages 10 and 11 by Ed Francis.

Published by Willowisp Press, Inc.
401 E. Wilson Bridge Road, Worthington, Ohio 43085

Copyright © 1989 by Willowisp Press, Inc.

Printed in the United States of America
10 9 8 7 6 5 4 3 2 1

ISBN 0-87406-431-7

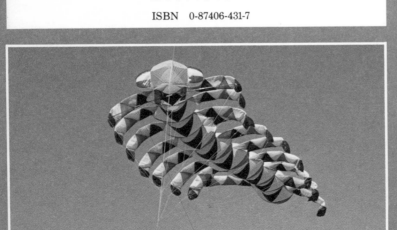

Table of Contents

Fun with Kites

Flying a kite makes you feel special. It is peaceful to hold a string attached to a kite as it floats high above the ground. Dave Debolt, a man who loved to fly kites, said, "A kite line is a stairway to heaven."

Kites are as old as the pyramids of Egypt and as new as the latest video game. Kites have been used in experiments and in saving people's lives. They also have been used in wars.

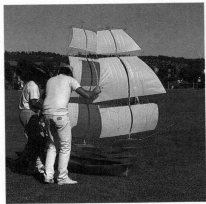

Kites come in different shapes. Some are shaped like diamonds. Others look like fish, dragonflies, or butterflies. Many people build their own kites and invent their own kite shapes.

Kite festivals are held around the world. Maybe some day you'll be lucky enough to see a kite festival. It's an unforgettable sight!

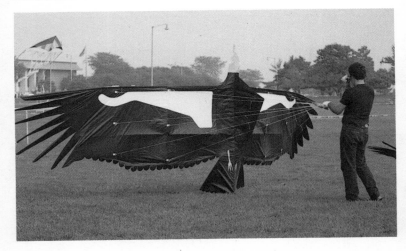

The First Kites

No one knows exactly when the kite was invented, but the first recorded kite flight was in China, about 200 B.C. That means the kite is more than 2000 years old. The kites on this page are copies of ancient Oriental kites.

The first use of the kite was probably in a war. Scary-looking kites or kites that made a sound when the wind rushed by them were used to frighten enemy armies. Some really big kites even carried soldiers into the air so they could shoot arrows down on the enemy. Imagine how you would feel if you were a soldier and you looked up to see a scary-looking kite with enemy soldiers shooting down at you!

Over the centuries, kite flying spread from China and Japan to Europe and then to North America. Now people all over the world have fun flying kites!

Kites in History

Many different people have used kites. Benjamin Franklin (top left) discovered electricity in the 1700s when he flew a kite during an electrical storm. Alexander Graham Bell (middle left), who invented the telephone, made very big kites. In 1907, one of his kites lifted a man almost 200 feet above the ground. The Wright brothers (bottom left) used kites to help design their plane.

Page 8 shows a picture of a steerable *target kite*. World War II artillery gunners used this kite for target practice. The *box kite,* shown next to the target kite, was used to help rescue pilots who had crashed. People flew the *barrage kite* (lower right, page 9) in front of enemy planes to make them crash.

Kites have had other uses, too. They have helped build bridges and rescue people at sea. People in Malaysia have even used kites to catch fish.

The Parts of a Kite

The *spar*, *strut*, *bridle*, and *sail* are parts of a kite. The spar is the piece that runs across the kite. It crosses the strut, which is the part that runs from the top of the kite to the bottom. The spar and strut form the *frame* of the kite.

The sail is the fabric that covers the frame of the kite. The bridle is the line that is always attached to the kite. It is the line that the main flying line is tied to. The place where the main flying line is tied to the bridle is called the *towing point*. It can be adjusted so the kite can fly in different wind conditions. The *tail* helps keep the kite from wobbling.

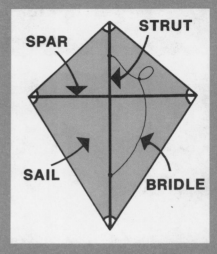

Kite Safety Rules

When you fly a kite, always follow the safety rules listed below.

- *Never fly your kite during a storm.*
- *Stay away from power lines.*
- *Don't fly your kite near airports or busy streets.*
- *Never use any metal parts in your kite, including wire.*
- *Watch out for trees—some eat kites!*

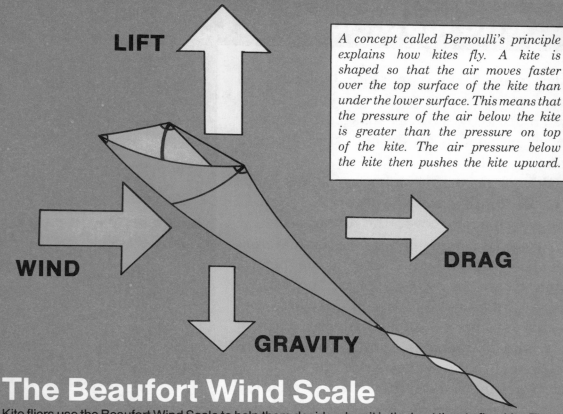

LIFT

WIND

DRAG

GRAVITY

A concept called Bernoulli's principle explains how kites fly. A kite is shaped so that the air moves faster over the top surface of the kite than under the lower surface. This means that the pressure of the air below the kite is greater than the pressure on top of the kite. The air pressure below the kite then pushes the kite upward.

The Beaufort Wind Scale

Kite fliers use the Beaufort Wind Scale to help them decide when it is the best time to fly a kite. The Beaufort Wind Scale measures how hard the wind is blowing. When the wind is blowing very hard, kite flying can be difficult. If the wind is not blowing hard enough, it may be hard to get a kite up into the air. Average kite fliers will find it easiest to fly their kites when the Beaufort Wind Scale is at 2, 3, or 4, as shown below.

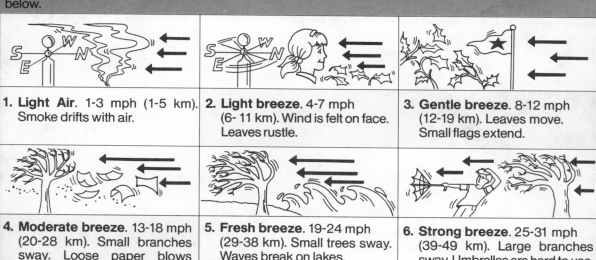

1. **Light Air.** 1-3 mph (1-5 km). Smoke drifts with air.

2. **Light breeze.** 4-7 mph (6- 11 km). Wind is felt on face. Leaves rustle.

3. **Gentle breeze.** 8-12 mph (12-19 km). Leaves move. Small flags extend.

4. **Moderate breeze.** 13-18 mph (20-28 km). Small branches sway. Loose paper blows around.

5. **Fresh breeze.** 19-24 mph (29-38 km). Small trees sway. Waves break on lakes.

6. **Strong breeze.** 25-31 mph (39-49 km). Large branches sway. Umbrellas are hard to use.

Kite Materials

For over 2,000 years, kite builders have had the same problem. They needed to know how to make kites that were light enough to fly and still strong enough to stay together.

Older kites had bamboo or other kinds of wood for the frame, and cloth (often silk) or paper to cover the frame.

But today many new kinds of materials have been developed. Some of the new materials are as light as paper, but are almost impossible to tear. Some kites use rip-stop nylon, the same material used in tents and parachutes.

The first kite strings were made of silk. Now, many kite fliers use synthetic strings. It's important to use string that is strong enough to stay attached to the kite as it is whipped by the wind.

The pieces of hardware, shown at the right, are often used by kite makers.

Paper, cotton, silk, and nylon are used to make the sail of the kite.

String can range from lightweight cord for small kites to heavy rope for very large kites.

Bamboo, rattan, and synthetic materials are sometimes used for the frame of the kite.

Kites, Kites, Kites!

Kites come in all shapes and sizes. People who build kites are only limited by their imaginations. Some of the different kinds of kites are delta, cellular, soft, and stunt. Some of the most amazing kites you'll ever see are the Oriental kites. These can be in the shapes of flying fish, soaring birds, or even long, wriggly insects!

Figure Kites

A kite doesn't have to look like a box, a diamond, or a triangle. A kite can look like lots of different things! The ancient Chinese made kites that looked like dragonflies and butterflies. The ancient Japanese painted faces on kites that looked like devils and famous warriors.

Modern kites can look like almost anything you can think of! That's what's so incredible about kites. As long as your kite flies, it can look like anything you want.

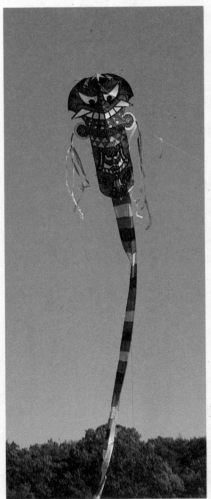

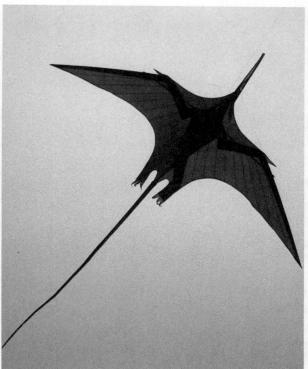

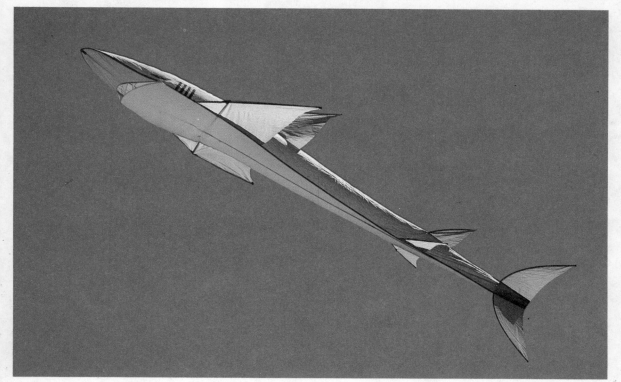

Trains

Trains are just as spectacular as Oriental kites. Trains are a series of kites which are all connected to the same string. The longest train kites have more than 1000 kites on one line! Trains can lift objects—even people—into the air.

Some kite trains look like dragons or centipedes, with tails that are almost as long as six airliners in a row!

Delta Kites

A *delta kite* is a special kind of kite that is used when there's not much breeze. Because of the way it is designed, this kind of kite can stay up when the wind is moving as slow as three miles per hour. The delta is a high-flying kite that is perfect for beginners. But it's still lots of fun for experienced kite fliers, too.

The delta is easy to make. You can even make a delta out of a plastic bag. It's shaped like a triangle. Some deltas don't even need a tail. As you can see from these pictures, deltas come in many different shapes and sizes.

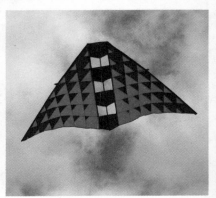

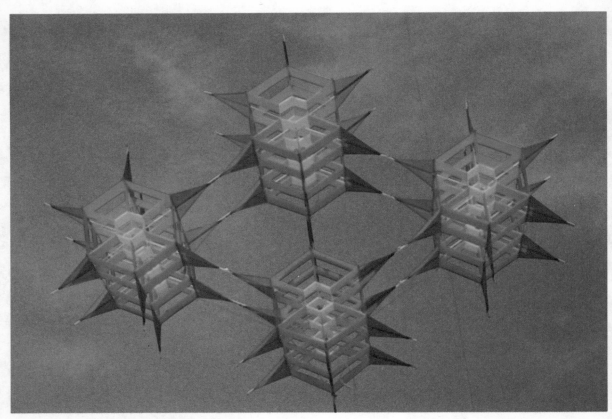

Cellular and Box Kites

The *cellular kite* is more complicated than the delta. It is a big kite made of many boxes, or cells. A cellular kite can look like the train engine below.

The *box kite* is a kind of cellular kite. The very first box kite was made in the late 1800s by Lawrence Hargrave of Australia. Early in this century, box kites were used by meteorologists—people who study weather. They hooked instruments to the kite and then sent it high into the air. The instruments on the kite gave them valuable information about weather conditions.

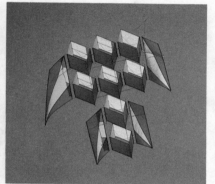

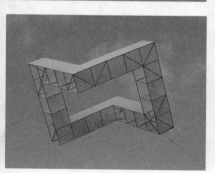

Soft Kites

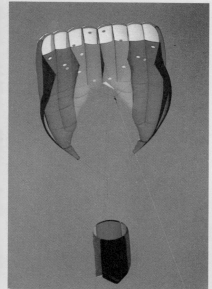

Look up in the sky! Is it a bird? A plane? Superman?

Well, no.

Is it a hot air balloon? A parachute? A giant beach ball?

No, it's a kite! Some kites don't need a stick frame. These kinds of kites are called *soft kites*, and they're a little like parachutes. Wind enters the kite through openings in the front, and the kite inflates like an air mattress.

Soft kites can be huge, but they're easy to carry around because they pack away into a bag.

Stunt Kites

There's no doubt about it!

The superstars of the kite world are the stunt kites. It's hard to learn how to fly stunt kites. But they're great to watch in action once you have learned how to fly them.

The key to flying a stunt kite is control. These kites have two or more flying lines, so they're a little like marionette puppets.

People who fly stunt kites have to learn how to make them turn just the right way at just the right time. The kites make loops, spins, and dives. As the picture below (right) shows, some stunt kites are strong enough to pull a person off of the ground!

Sometimes many people fly stunt kites together. There are special events for people who like to fly stunt kites.

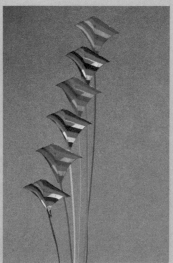

Accessories

Accessories make flying kites even more fun. One kind of accessory is called sky junk. Sky junk (p. 29) is decorations that are attached to kite lines.

You've probably seen a wind sock hanging on a pole on somebody's porch or patio. Wind socks look like tubes of bright fabric. Kite fliers hang these on their lines. Some are as long as ten cars lined up bumper to bumper.

A *kite climber* is a round or cone-shaped piece of paper or bamboo that is hung on the line. The wind sends it hurling up toward the kite. Some kite climbers even make noise as they zoom up the kite line.

Other accessories, such as *reels* (this page), help keep kite lines from getting tangled.

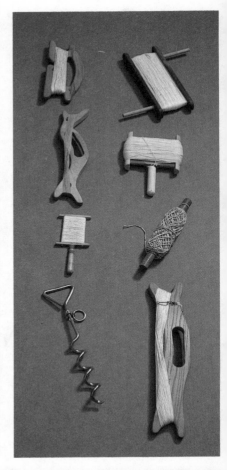

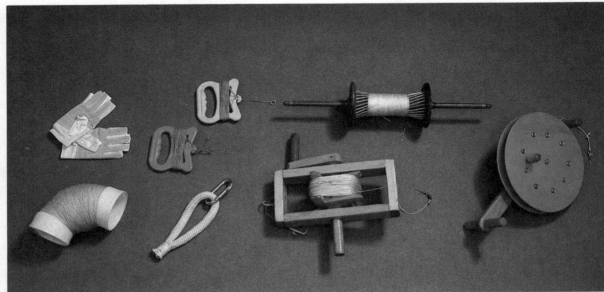

Festivals

There are many kite flying festivals. Watch your local newspaper to see if a festival is coming to your town or city. Make sure you phone ahead before planning a trip.

Here are two addresses to write to if you want to know more about kites and kite flying.

American Kitefliers Association
1559 Rockville Pike
Rockville, Maryland 20852
USA

British Kite Flying Association
P.O. Box 35
Hemel Hempstead, Herts, HP1 1EE
England

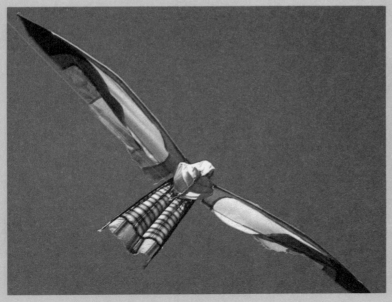

Glossary of Kite Terms

barrage kite—flown to get in the way of enemy planes and make them crash

box kite—a four-sided kite, a type of cellular kite

bridle—line attached to the kite to set the angle of flight

cellular kite—several box kites linked together to make a big kite

delta kite—a lightweight, easy-to-make kite that's good for beginners

frame—the "bones" or structure of a kite

kite climber—a decoration that climbs the line up to the kite

reels—the spool that the line is wound around

sail—fabric that covers the frame of the kite

soft kite—a kite without a frame, similar to a parachute

spar—piece of the frame that runs across the kite

strut—piece of the frame that runs up and down the kite

tail—long piece of fabric, tied to the bottom, that helps stabilize the kite

towing point—the place where the main flying line is tied to the bridle

train—several kites of the same size attached to one line

target kite—used by World War II gunners for target practice

Index